ENDORSEMENTS

"A thoughtful guide that provides a practical, direct approach to exploring the complex issues of wealth with children and young adults. Wish I had this book when my kids were younger!"

—MADELEINE ARNOW, Arnow Family Foundation

"Families of wealth struggle with many of the issues that all families face—but the wealth acts as an amplifier. The issue of the wealth itself, and what it means or doesn't mean to each family member is so often a paralyzing issue. This refreshing book by Barbara and Suzy encourages parents to stay focused on the more important issues—of love and respect for the children and each other."

—DIRK JUNGE, a member of the Pitcairn family
(and Executive Chairman of the Board)

Sigmund Freud advises that money is the greatest impediment to happiness as no nice person will talk about it. Having the "money" talk, like having the "sex" talk, is a subject very few look forward to and even fewer do well. Barbara and Suzy enable that talk—making it joyful and doable.

—JAMES E. HUGHES, JR., author of Family: The Compact
Among Generations and The Cycle of the Gift

In this delightful—and playfully illustrated—book, authors Barbara Hauser and Suzan Peterfriend offer much-needed advice for affluent parents concerned about the effect of wealth on their children.

Expanding on their prior book, which focused the discussion on children aged five, this version offers practical suggestions for how to have the "money" conversation with children aged 12 and 20. Tackling sensitive questions such as "Where does money come from?" and "If Daddy divorces us, can I still go to camp this summer?", the book gives parents sample language to use in their responses and a framework for sharing their value systems about family finances.

Understanding that family money and its impact on children transcends borders, the authors also share their insights about families in Asia, Latin America and the Gulf Region.

Mommy, Are We Rich? is a must-read for parents seeking meaningful dialogue with their children about this extremely critical topic.

—Dawn S. Markowitz, Esq., legal editor, *Trusts & Estates* magazine

The disconnection in awareness between affluent parents and their children is immense, and unfortunately, their ability to understand each other and hold a productive conversation about family money and wealth is limited. The consequence of this is much unhappiness, misunderstanding and missed opportunities for productive exchange and good decisions and life choices.

This book takes a child's eye view of the meaning of money and wealth, and helps parents become aware of how thoughtful, concerned and yes, sophisticated and aware, their children are. It shows the way to open up a dialogue across generations, and how even the youngest member of a family can and should be engaged.

By sharing stories and works from young people, this book is completely unique and uniquely useful.

—Dennis Jaffe, Ph.D., Professor and author of *Stewardship In Your Family Enterprise: Developing Responsible Family Leadership Across Generations*

There exists a cottage industry of advisors whose job seems to be to confirm many of parents' worst fears about money and their children. Barbara and Suzan dispose of all that and bring a vision based on long experience that sees wealth for what it really is: a powerful tool for us and those we care for to imagine and to pursue our most profound dreams. The idea of wealth as a sickness, *affluenza,* is set aside. The shame with which North American culture regards inherited wealth is put in the perspective of different cultures, and gives parents a chance to embrace higher, universal values.

As a result "Mommy, are we rich?" is not simply empty talking points for parents containing ideas they don't truly believe themselves.

This book is for the one-percenters who want, in joy and not shame, to leave a beautiful legacy for themselves, for their children, and for the planet.

—Eugene Lipitz, CIO of the family office Commodore Management and author of the essay "Daddy, are we rich?"

Mommy, are we  Rich?

Talking to
Children About
Family Money

(ages 5 & 12 & 20)

Barbara R. Hauser
& Suzan Peterfriend

Published by Mesatop Press
Minneapolis, MN 55401

Printed by Gorham Printing Centralia, Washington

First edition ISBN 0-9706026-1-8
Second edition ISBN 978-0-9706026-7-1

Library of Congress Control Number: 2001117763

With Appreciation to

The kind and generous individuals who shared
so many personal experiences

&

The Family Advisory Council

(with special thanks to our artists,
Ali Oshinsky, at age 4 [in the original edition],
granddaughter Taylor Senter [age 12] and
granddaughter Lucile Hauser Cameron [age 13])

(Suzy also thanks Leslie Rozencwaig for sharing his wisdom)

Dedicated to

Children everywhere
(including our grandchildren now)

With love and encouragement
As they learn about the world and themselves

2014 Preface

When we wrote "Mommy, are we Rich?" in 2001, times were good. The global financial crisis was seven years later.

Wealthy families were worried: not about the wealth itself, but about the effect that wealth would have on their children. The question asked over and over was "When should we tell them about the money?"

Why were parents so worried? We think there were two reasons. The first was about "incentives" (children would not have the incentive to work hard if they knew they were rich.) The second was that not only would they not be motivated, but worse they would have a sense of "entitlement."

After the global financial crisis, this concern faded for a while—families were more concerned about the safety of their wealth. Now it seems that globally wealthy families are feeling more secure about their wealth, and turning their attention again to the children, and the effect the wealth might have on their children.

Everyone has asked us for help with "older" children also, so we have expanded this book to include 12-year-olds and 20-year-olds. (Someone already asked if we can cover the 30-year-olds next time). In the first edition our focus was on the United States. Since that time Barbara has continued her global travels and found that parents everywhere had the same concerns. During that time Suzy has been increasingly sought after by Latin families who were establishing U.S. connections. They needed advice also, and had the same concerns as all other wealthy parents. Looking back we can conclude today that those concerns are truly universal. We have added global "nuances" for each chapter. Our goal, always, is to help parents everywhere enjoy raising happy and confident children.

We hope former and new readers and parents will find this expanded version useful, reassuring and helpful.

Barbara & Suzy

The 2009 International Update

When we wrote this book, in 2001, the focus was the United States, because the issue was so widespread among U.S. parents. In a "new" country, the lack of familiarity with family wealth was causing anxiety. The questions in many homes and in seminars were "How much is too much?" and "When do I tell the children about the money?" and "What do I say if they ask if we are rich?"

These same issues seem to be spreading around the world. In 2006, a second generation son in Saudi Arabia asked me to tell his father that a benefit of the family wealth was that the son could pursue one of his academic dreams (See chapter 8 and "how much money does a ballerina get?"). In 2007, a *Wall Street Journal* reporter in New Delhi phoned me. Parents in India were worried about the impact of recent family wealth on their children. "Our children are growing up with…air conditioning, and shopping malls." In 2008, an English father with a long history of family wealth described his own efforts to teach his children to become self-reliant, just in case. In 2009, a father in Switzerland confided his worry: "Our young children know only five-star hotels." The words are different; the concerns are the same.

Not all countries share the "Puritan" work ethic that is so strong in the United States (where "unearned" money is somehow suspect) but all parents seem to worry about how to talk to their children about family money.

My own focus has increasingly been beyond the United States and I encounter these parental concerns more and more often, wherever I am. I hope that this new printing will reach many readers outside of the United States, and I look forward to more comments.

Barbara Hauser

(BRHauser@gmail.com)

Introduction

Why read this book?

If you have children or grandchildren, or work with families who are involved with issues of family wealth—we have written this book for you. After decades of our own work with wealthy families, as a trusts and estates lawyer and as someone involved with family wealth preservation centered around tailored life insurance products, as well as strategic advisors to financial institutions, we decided we needed to stop and write this book. Why? Because everywhere we went parents and grandparents would come up to us with questions about *how* and *when* to say *what* to children about "the money."

We have many stories of sudden disclosure on the eve of premarital agreements, or as the first trust distributions were made. We have also seen far too many young adults deeply confused about how to live their own lives with a poorly understood background of family wealth.

Everyone asked: "Isn't there a book we could read to help us?" We couldn't find any.

As parents ourselves, we kept thinking that the right time to begin talking with children about money was at a very early age—as soon as they asked any questions at all. Then the communications could continue, in a natural and positive way, throughout the growing-up years. So we chose age 5 for the child who asks questions in this book. It's a good age because it is the cross-over for them into a wider outside group of peers and others, and it's an age when they are busy asking questions about everything under the sun.

In the chapter discussions, you will see that we are careful to bring out into the open many of the "difficult" issues underlying these simple questions. Then we go on to show some very positive answers you can give, answers that will reinforce all of your own family values.

We have been fortunate to work with so many families around the world, including families whose names have long been identified with "wealth," who have learned how to use their family wealth with a caring love for each other and for the wider world around them.

We thank them for the insights we are glad to share with all of you who read this book.

Family wealth can be simply one more aspect of a family and its children, values and enjoyment. We hope you enjoy the book!

—*Barbara & Suzy*

(We would love to hear from you; emails are Suzypfross@aol.com and BRHauser@gmail.com)

Contents

CHAPTER ONE

The Feared Question

"Mommy, are we rich?" Parents all around the world are afraid to answer this question. Why?

Parents have become frozen about the right way to answer that question. They want to be good parents. But money has such a "sullied" meaning in most societies that there seems to be no good answer.

The first reaction to the question is a natural reluctance and defensiveness. For reasons we'll discuss in the next chapter, parents everywhere are uneasy about being seen as "rich" and they are afraid that if their children think they are "rich," then the children will grow up to be lazy and self-indulgent. As parents, no one wants that to happen to their children.

- To answer falsely "No, we are not" is to lie to children and lose credibility and trust as a parent, which is something that may never be regained.

- To "fudge" about the answer sends a message of confusion as in: "Yes, we are rich. We have many of the blessings of life, and health and family." or "We might seem so, but not really rich, not like other people."

They will pick up the confusion and uncertainty, and if that does not change as they grow up, they will pass on the same murkiness to their own children.

To criticize a child for asking the question is perhaps the harshest message of all. That child will learn that there is one forbidden subject in the family.

What do children think?

One youngster could only figure out that maybe "being rich" meant making cans for vegetables.

(The answer to his question about whether they had "lots of money" was to show him a can of products that were similar to ones grown on some of their farms. All he was shown, though, was the can, so for many years he thought they must own the company that made the cans!)

To a child this question, of simple curiosity, is asked in innocence, like so many other questions.

But to a parent this particular question generates genuine anxiety about finding the best possible answer. So the answers given to the child are filled with so many complexities that the child is likely to be more confused by the answers!

Why?

We think we know why. We both are parents and we love the importance of children in our lives. Our professional lives have involved working with family wealth of many sizes, held by many generations, and inevitably causing tough family issues.

Sex is simple to talk about, next to money!

The simple answers in this book are to reassure parents, that—like sex—money can be talked about in a natural and truthful way, in age-appropriate responses. Psychologists are well aware that the former taboos on talking about sex are gone but the ones about money are alive and well.

Our hope is that a return to the values of trust and frankness with young children will prevent many of the problems, hurts and insecurities we have seen in older children, young adults and actually in adults of all ages. Money does not have to be such a tough issue.

What is it about money anyway??

Age 12:

At age 12, in this information age, the child is ready to ask more serious questions. The question "Mommy, are we rich?" cannot be brushed aside. This is a very inquisitive age; the child is accumulating and processing more information than we ever did at that age.

The wishful thinking of many parents that "if we don't tell them, they won't know" is like a fantasy.

Again, though, we have consistent advice: try to ask why they are asking, and what is on their minds, so that you can give a meaningful answer (and start a healthy dialogue about wealth).

We have been amazed at the internal logic children this age have worked out. When asked "What do you want to be when you grow up?" one 12-year-old girl replied "Actually I do have a rather big plan. I want to be a brand, for clothes and make-up, but to do that I first have to get famous, so I will be an actress."

This is a great age to ask "What do you want to be when you grow up?" and tie that in to money. "How much money do you think you will need to be able to do that?"

One boy (son of a lawyer) had already adjusted his life plan, based on money. He said he really wanted to be a baseball player when he grew up, but his Dad has explained that he would not be earning very much money. He shifted his goal to becoming a lawyer, one who would specialize in baseball players and help them with their contracts.

We don't know if his father understood how disappointed his son had become, and if they were able to talk about it. The boy was clearly getting the message that money was more important than his happiness. (see our Ballerina chapter).

Age 20:

This is an age when the young adult has a serious need to prepare for the future. Whether there is family wealth, and whether it is "available" to the child is a very important question. It can affect choices about education and planned life styles.

This time the answer can lead into balance sheets. It is time that they understand how finances work. If there are family trusts, this is a time to explain how those trusts will work: who makes decisions about distributions and what guidelines do they follow. It is also smart to disclose any automatic distribution ages.

Finally, it is likely to be an age of considering a life partner. If there will be unequal amounts of wealth this is a great time to begin explaining how different couples (including their parents) treat wealth issues. Are all of the assets pooled together? Are some kept in separate names? Is there a safety fund somewhere? What are your views about prenuptial agreements? What are their views?

One 60-year-old still remembers that when she was 20, with very wealthy parents, her mother constantly told her "You must be capable of supporting yourself, just in case you ever need to."

GLOBAL NUANCES:

Asian (with a particular focus on ethnic Chinese)

Asian families may be particularly reluctant to share any information about family wealth. Again, this does not at all mean that the child has no other information resources.

By not talking frankly about the wealth, the family continues a tradition of secrecy that often leads to family litigation. They are also very worried about the negative effect the wealth may have on their children. They worry that when young children learn they are wealthy, they will easily become spoiled, lazy and develop a selfish sense of entitlement.

Latin

Latin families value their extended families so much that there is more often an attitude of inclusion (not secrecy). The elders want to share the information. They trust their children, and see it as part of taking care of them. They are also extremely concerned, in certain countries, about the physical risks (kidnap, murder) that their wealth can attract, concerns they discuss with their children. One father who moved to Florida explained "We can now sleep by open windows."

They appreciate the conversations about family wealth and what it means to each of them.

Gulf

Gulf families may be less concerned about hiding family wealth. In many cases, the head of the family controls all of the family wealth and the children are accustomed to having someone else take care of their needs. They are aware of the poor (Shariah law requires an annual gift to the poor of 2.5% of the family's annual net worth) but they tend to socialize with other families that have wealth very similar to their own.

As with newly wealthy families, in any country, this is an especially acute concern when the parents themselves did not grow up in a wealthy family. The parents were not taught how to live with family wealth: it was not a topic.

Now that the parents are wealthy, they do not know how to teach their children to grow up wisely with the wealth. The assumptions other children will make (based on their parents' opinions) are often negative and even based on envy.

Children everywhere need to learn that the wealth does not define who they are as people. Parents everywhere need to concentrate on raising children who are confident and competent (and not get distracted by the wealth).

CHAPTER TWO

Americans are Weird About Money!

"Anyone who isn't confused doesn't
really understand the situation."

—EDWARD R. MURROW

Americans have been confused about money from the beginning. It all started with the Puritans, who have had a tremendous influence on us all. Idleness was a punishable crime.

The Puritans knew:"Idleness is the work of the devil."

The famous founders of our country believed in a religious and moral sense that wasting time was a serious "sin."

Did you know that in the Bay Colony (Massachusetts), in 1633, the following was actually a crime:

"No person, householder or other, shall spend his time idly or un-profitably, under pain of such punishment as the court shall think meet to inflict; and for this end it is ordered, that the constables of every place shall use special diligence to take knowledge of offenders of this kind, especially of common coasters, unprofitable fowlers and tobacco takers, and to present the same."

This gives you a sense of the tenor of the times. We want to stress this history because we believe that the unconscious inheritance of these same values is the source of a great deal of anxiety. Why?

Ben Franklin taught us all about the need to put in an "honest day's work." By working hard and being thrifty we can amass wealth and achieve the American Dream.

And if we don't "work" for a living, then there's something inferior or even immoral about us? (You need to know here—we completely disagree with this!!)

So we have the work ethic ingrained in our society. So much so that anyone who does not "work for a living" is often looked down upon. In the writings to support our high estate tax, you can find expressions of amazing scorn for the "idle rich" who were born with the proverbial silver spoon. We even grew up with the expression "filthy rich." Here's one writer's scornful description of wealthy heirs, which is about as bad as we've ever seen.

> *"[Inherited wealth] all too often leaves [heirs] broken and debauched ....Supine on expensive piles of pillows, they receive injections of more legal drugs from elegant doctor feelgoods. . . ."*

So, there is an ingrained belief in most of the American culture that to be good people we must work hard for a living. We Americans are the ones who went on (in 1971) to coin the word "workaholic." Enjoyment was irrelevant.

By the way, the younger generation (Generation X) doesn't see this the same way. Their response to the workaholic preoccupation is:"Get a life!" They are trying to make more room for family time, and they are busy having babies!

But the Boomers, who are creating unprecedented wealth, are not so clear about how to fit the wealth into their lives. Even the younger dot. com millionaires are being studied and written about in terms of another new word—"affluenza."

We think it is no coincidence that the source of the word "affluenza" is a bad illness? Worse yet is the coined phrase "sudden wealth syndrome" which has undertones of death in it!

We disagree with all of this, strongly. Why should wealth— itself a neutral material— be viewed as an illness or even death? Let us accept wealth as a means to accomplish some wonderful good in the world.

We know many wealthy families who:

- Raise polite and kind children—with love and trust across the generations
- Work hard and productively all the time, and not for a salary
- Pass on a family legacy of generosity

(A happy family!)

So—wealth does *not* have to been viewed as:

- catching an illness, as "affluenza" and it is *not*
- being at risk for your very life, with a "sudden wealth syndrome."

Wealth is just money—it can be used to make you and your children very happy.

Now that we've shown why this is a confusing subject—and maybe harder to talk about than sex—let's look at the questions little children are apt to ask.

We'll begin at the beginning.

Global nuances

Asian

For newly wealthy Asian families (including successful Chinese business owners) there is often a hunger to buy famous brands, and lots of them. New to the wealthy world they have become avid art collectors. They are buying homes in several countries. Their children are going to smart boarding schools.

Latin

There is a general aversion to "showy" wealth, especially when the home country life is filled with safety concerns (kidnapping and murder). Visible consumption becomes dangerous. In a more private setting, they have pleasure in acquiring art and have some lovely private collectibles. Having family wealth is a very mixed blessing. In some cases the adjustment to a sudden lack of formerly "unlimited" wealth is a difficult one.

Gulf

Gulf families are dealing with large amounts of wealth, and are paying attention to family issues. The well-being of the entire extended family has a very high value.

One sheik in Bahrain explained his views: "If the wealth causes any friction in my family, I will give it all away."

One wealthy Saudi mother explained: "If you lose your money, you can always get more money. But if you lose your brother, you will not get another brother."

CHAPTER THREE

"What is Money?"

We all know that babies come from the stork. Kids today all know that money comes from machines!

Our first point, when children ask questions like this, is to keep the basics in mind. Remember all the jokes about the long detailed biological answers to the question of where baby brother came from, with the punch line being the child's clarification that her friend's baby brother came from King's Hospital, so where did her brother come from?

Find out what the child really does want to know, and give a simple but truthful answer that meets those needs.

It's really not any different than the questions about the birds and the bees. Little children will pick up their own ideas, some of them quite amusing. But this is a good place to start the pattern of simple answers to simple questions on the continuing topic of wealth.

So, what is money? We have collected answers from some five-year-olds. One child has it just right.

"Money is what you use to pay for things."

Children can see and touch "money" which makes this the easiest question in the conversation you will be having about wealth in many ways.

It's also fun to show children money from other countries, if you have some around from trips, etc. This would have expanded the views of the child who said "money is green with peoples' faces on it." We think that child would have fun seeing the pink, blue, purple and orange bills from other countries.

One standard source for definitions is always the dictionary.

What does an Oxford American Dictionary say? It begins with:

> **"Money is coin. Portable pieces of stamped metal used as a medium of exchange. Coins and banknotes...amount of money is wealth". . .and**—believe it or not—"marry money" is there too, and explained as to "marry a rich person"!

The central meaning of money is its use as a "medium of exchange." Money then can be exchanged for many other items.

One child understands the basics of this. His answer was: "Money is what you need for everything."

Later, we will discuss some of the entrenched negatives associated with that concept of exchange (money can buy influence, control, pardons, power, love and so on). But now we will be pointing out the positives that can come from exchange.

We will include the basics: *spending, saving* and *giving.*

Your answers at this point could include several of these positive statements:

> **#1—"Money is what we all use to *pay* for things. Instead of trading an apple for a lollipop, we sell the apple for money, and then we can use that money to buy the lollipop or to buy something else."** *(This covers the general, "medium of exchange" meaning of money).*
>
> **#2—"Money is something we try to *save*, so we have it if we need some later."**

To parents: Children will have a hard time with this—as many parents know quite well! We think this is because they don't yet understand where money comes from.

By the way, though, did you think about what it means that the word used for saving money ("save") is the same word as in "save from danger"? Many tycoons still save scrupulously to prevent danger in the future. Those who remember the Depression era, even if only from their parents, are afraid it could happen again. This brings up the "dark side" of reasons for saving: the dangers, risks, uncertainties and insecurities—which are hard topics for small children.

[Note: We asked our artist to make a scary drawing to put in here, but she did not want to scare anyone: "If any children see it they would go hide under the bed, so I won't."]

At this point, it might be enough to give an example of saving some small amounts in order to have enough to buy something they want that costs more.

For example, "if you don't buy a lollipop every day you will save enough to buy the teddy bear you want." The drawback from using this kind of example is that it keeps the focus on consumption, which is only one reason that we save.

It might be enough then, to give that example, and to add "and there are other reasons we save too."

Some of the other topics will be appropriate responses when children are older.

Interestingly, even at a young age children begin to equate saving with feeling rich.

"My piggybank is full. I am rich."

And some just pick up the love of saving. "I love to keep it."

#3—"Money is something we *give*, to people who need it."

Of course there are lots of different kinds of "need." Children can see the man on the street asking for money; they might be taught at preschool or from the family's religion that it is just expected to give money from time to time although they might not understand where it goes very well.

The Oxford American Dictionary defines "need" as a "lack of necessaries."

A child's view of "necessaries" can be cute!

"You have to give it to people, at least enough for them to buy stuff to play with."

More seriously, it isn't too hard to explain that not all people have enough for the basic necessities: food, clothing and shelter. In fact, many families like to include children in supporting food banks, soup kitchens, building Habitats for Humanity, etc.

Contributions to civic causes, such as the arts, schools, camps and hospitals can also be used to explain special ways a family might like to give, and why.

The Oxford American Dictionary defines "contributions" as "giving jointly with others" and "helping to bring about. . . ."

Children can see the family name, as one among many, in symphony programs, or on donors' lists on walls. See our discussion later in the book for examples of how family philanthropy can be a way of teaching children about family values.

LESSON

Once again, it's back to the basics.

- Raise children to have their family values,

- Raise children to be careful and kind,

- Raise children to be wise with the wealth—

- *and* answer their questions, all of them, simply and with loving honesty.

Before moving on though, we have to include the dear quote from one little child, who has money all figured out. Here's her definition.

One five-year-old cut right to the end: "Money is being rich."

Now that we know what money is, the next question from a child is "Where does money come from?"

Age 12:

This is an age when they can start count-ing their money. They are learning how to shop. They are very interested in the cost of everything.

This is a great age to increase their allowance. Allowances are a lesson in budgeting. They may be talking to their peers, and asking for an increase in al-lowance. Pay attention to their reasons, and enjoy another opportunity for a great conversation about family values around money issues.

Many families negotiate with their 12-year-olds: "If you really want that item that costs more than you have saved, we will pay half and you pay half." That is a great lesson about co-investing!

One boy that age was receiving an allowance for his "extras." The par-ents were paying for all of his clothes. At one of their weekly family meet-ings he asked to have his allowance increased enough so that he would also buy his own clothes. They agreed. After two months he came back and asked "Could I go back to the smaller allowance, and you buy my clothes? It's too complicated to do it this way."

Age 20:

At age 20 the meaning of money is tied directly into the life choices that the young adult is making. Some parents engage the child in a life-plan-ning discussion. "How do you want to be living when you are age 40?"

"How much money will it take to live that way?" "What are your plans to have that amount?"

A Latin 20-year-old knew what the family wealth meant in her life: "I can go to the best schools, my family will pay any amounts for schools. Then the rest is up to me."

One 20-year-old American was scheduled to receive a trust distribution at age 21 of tens of millions. He had some deeply thoughtful conversations with the family advisor and his parents, and decided to divert the distribution to a new 10-year trust, which he would receive at age 30.

He explained: "These are the 10 years when I will work the hardest to achieve my life planning goals. I don't want the temptation of doing nothing, because of the money."

GLOBAL NUANCES

Asian

For the newly wealthy, the money means opportunities everywhere. The wealth allows any number of luxury purchases. As we will see in the "Sammy" chapter, this can also lead to some competitiveness. The wealth also makes it possible for Asian families to create some very charitable organizations, especially for health and education. They may also become substantial donors of schools their children attend.

Latin

For those families that have relocated to the United States, the families have often had to cope with a sudden lack of easy wealth. The children may have no servants surrounding them. They will not be traveling with guards, in armored cars. Just like the need to learn a faster fluency in English the whole family needs to learn a new language about wealth. Not only is their net worth diminished, the U.S. taxes are often a surprise. They need to adjust to new societal attitudes about being wealthy. It no longer is a scary beacon to kidnappers. Diamond earrings can be worn with pleasure, not fear.

Gulf

Since the oil boom in the 1970s Gulf families have become accustomed to family wealth. They still revere their family history, and will often brag about their ancestor, who started with only a camel. As with Asian families that are newly wealthy, they can enjoy the ability to own and enjoy luxuries, large and small.

CHAPTER FOUR

"Where does money come from?"

The dictionary won't help with this one (except for the cute definition of marrying money!).

Where do children think money comes from?

We grew up hearing a lot about where money does NOT come from. "Money does not grow on trees." That ruled out one option, but didn't add much useful information. By the way that idea seems to live on.

One five-year-old knew:

"Money comes from trees."

As with many questions like this from children, why not respond by asking them first—where do they think it comes from? Then you will know the child's frame of reference and current "understanding."

Here are some of the places young children think money comes from.

"Money comes from a machine."

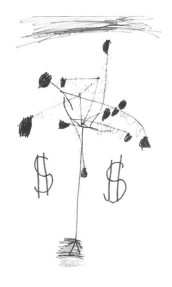

This was the clear winner. Almost all of the children gave this as their first answer. But there are other insightful answers too.

A watchful boy decided.

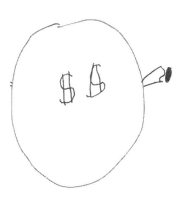

"Money comes from money trucks."

Another had guessed that by analogy, if everything else comes from a store, then money must also.

"Money comes from the money store."

Some have seen it handed back in all kinds of stores, and haven't quite figured out the connection.

"The store gives you back money when you give them some."

One connection parents would like to make, along the lines of money not growing on trees, is that it takes some kind of work to have money. A few children do know this early on.

"Money comes from working."

On the other hand, the "working" connection might not be as clear to them as you assume it is. One child connected it with the office, but that was it.

"Money comes from Daddy's office."

Some have been paying attention to where their parents go to get more money. One child gave as the alternate to a "machine" a trip to the bank.

"When you run out of money you just go to
the bank and they give you more."

Finally, we love the child who has a grasp of the generational positions in family wealth.

"Money comes from Grandpa."

See our later chapter on gifts from Grandparents!

So, what do you say about where money comes from?

LESSON

How about a general answer: "It comes from a lot of different places."

- Some money comes from *working*.

- Some money comes from *gifts*.

Some money comes from *saved money* that turns into more money, through investments.

P.S. As always, we should never underestimate the children. If we think that earnings on investments are too hard to explain to a five-year-old, we're probably wrong. We know for a fact that some have already figured it out on their own. As one smart little kid thought through his answer to "Where does money come from?" this is what he came up with.

"You know. . . having money gets you more money."

Age 12

When asked "Where does money come from?" one boy said he watched their business employees buying homes and raising families with the money: "It all comes from my father."

Even at that young age, many children think the money does come from credit cards. One child explained "I would rather have a credit card because it always has money, and the real money from my allowance is gone when I shop."

We overheard one mother on the phone to her shopping child: "The card does not have that much money in it." Asked to explain, "The card is tied to our real money, it does not have any itself unless we put some of our money in it."

Yet another young girl has figured out credit cards—and she wants to use a debit card—because it always has money (and, she explains, it doesn't come out of your allowance.)

Age 20

In a family that has a multi-generational business, the young people tend to assume it will always be there to take care of them. They don't bother to understand how the business works, and what actually produces the income.

This makes them poorly prepared to start their own ventures, or to invest wisely in others' business ventures.

We have recommended that young people in that situation should consider applying for loan from a bank to enable them to start a new business. The bank will require a solid written business plan, and will monitor the business, especially if the loan payments are not made on time. The young adult can learn much more from this experience than from asking a parent for the money.

Global nuances

Asia

Especially for the newly wealthy Asians, they know very well where the money comes from. They have worked to get it. They are fine about lavish spending because they can afford it and they are enjoying it. It is when there are generation transitions that the division of family wealth can cause so many well-publicized fights.

Latin

Many of the Latin families have wealth that "is just there" and has been for generations. It is used to support an extended family and in contributions to social needs. It is also used to continue to support adult children. If a young couple needs a home, the parents will buy it for them. It's all part of "just knowing" that there is family wealth that has always been there.

Sometimes adult daughters choose to manage personal accounts that are separate from their husbands, having grown up understanding the value of having a separate financial base.

Gulf

It is sometimes hard to see where the family wealth in the Gulf comes from. In simple terms, the oil revenues are received (largely) by the King, Sultan, Emir or Prime Minister. The ruler then undertakes massive infrastructure projects, carried out by a family business, which makes a profit.

Within the extended family it is often "the Uncles" who actually control the business and the family wealth. Those family businesses generate some 90% of the non-oil revenue of each country. The families do know where their money comes from, and they are very motivated to take good care of those businesses: to manage them well and to keep their entrepreneurial spirit strong.

CHAPTER FIVE

"Sammy says his parents have three houses. How many do we have?"

How would you answer this question? *If you have an easy simple answer, you can go ahead to the next chapter.*

We find that this is a question that can generate:

- anxiety

- confusion

- insecurities

Sammy's parents might feel awkward and embarrassed (even guilty!) that he said such a thing.

Let's look at this from Sammy's point of view. Is Sammy keeping score?

Or is Sammy asking a simple informational question?

Money is often used as a "scorecard." Sometimes this is a natural outcome of measuring "how far have you come?" Our culture does admire those who begin on their own and race ahead earning markers along the way. They may turn those markers into the latest car or a bigger house.

Having money can be a very abstract idea for children. They can count, though. They can count cars, houses, and anything else they can see and talk about.

In small towns, it is hard to "hide." Everyone can see who lives where, and what the house is like, and count the cars. One father praised Manhattan as a place where you can be more "anonymous."

Children know that one use of money is to accumulate goods. As one youngster explained it:

"Money helps you buy stuff."

Money does not have to always be a scorecard. It does not always have to be used to "buy stuff." As a member of one well-known family enjoys asking, in his talks about philanthropy—"How many yachts can you use anyway?"

On the other hand, some people do derive a pleasure from their collections: art, cars, model trains or yachts. In England people adore having collections of antique cars—and you can only use one car at a time. Another family has kept and displays all the art that an ancestor brought in an escape from Europe.

Albert Einstein, the great genius, remarked:

"Not everything that can be counted counts, and
not everything that counts can be counted."

So, how do you answer that question about how many [fill in the term] do we own?

LESSON

Why not explain the simple truth:

- "We have [correct number]."

- "Some people have more, some people have less."

If your child seems interested in more information, you could continue:

- "Some people like to spend their money on [e.g. houses, cars, etc.], some like to spend it on [whatever], and there are some people who don't like to spend it, they like to save it all."

- "We like to spend some of our money on [trips, or whatever] and we like to save some, too."

- "Some people have a lot of money sometimes and not so much money other times."

Age 12:

This chapter is about comparisons (and envy and bragging). Children at age 12 understand these comparisons. They can also read the Forbes 500 or the London "Rich list" online. Do they envy the families higher on the lists? Do they brag to families lower on the list?

Sometimes this attitude by parents gets played out in their children. One Texan father complained so strongly about his daughter's being invited to a friend's birthday—by private jet to New York for manicures—that it began to sound like envy of the friend's father, who clearly had "more."

The father swore it was about his disapproval of the other family's values. What if he had taken this opportunity to discuss his views with his daughter?

A more secure Gulf father shared a harmless bit of humor. His daughter had come from a friend's home and asked "Why don't we have ponies?" He joked, "Because we don't have a barn," and they both laughed.

One 12-year-old who had been busy making categories (which of his friends were rich, etc.) came home from school with a telling question. "Mommy," he said, "am I at a school for rich kids or a school for bright kids?" This layered question is another example of comparisons and trying to figure out where he fit in.

Age 20:

The most difficult issue will usually come up in the early 20's "What if my intended spouse has [much less] [much more] wealth than I do?" "Should we have a prenuptial agreement?"

Most laws about prenuptial require a full disclosure to each other of all of their assets. This often prompts the emotional response: "Do you think I am marrying you just for your money!" In this case it isn't about envy or bragging, it's about resentment or embarrassment (resulting from the comparison).

The media does not help. There are floods of articles about "the wealthiest [families in the United States][families anywhere][bachelors under 40] [under 30] etc. Global banks court future customers from the lists.

In 2014 even the White House participated in singling out those near the top of the list for some very special treatment. The "top 100 young philanthropists [read "wealthy"]" were invited to a private gathering at the White House. The *New York Times* article (complete with names and photos) called them "an elite group of 100 young philanthropists and heirs to billionaire family fortunes."

This is an opportunity to explain that the "family" wealth is special and does not belong to one child—it is a legacy in the larger family, to be nurtured and passed on for future generations, not to be carelessly dissipated. Remind them that the real value of a person is not connected to the family wealth. It comes from developing a secure sense of self-worth, which can be a value for both members of a couple.

Global Nuances

Asia

There are websites that rank countries by wealth. On one list (http://www. worldsrichestcountries.com) China, India and Japan hold rankings 2, 3 and 4. The next ranked Asian countries—South Korea, Indonesia and Taiwan are still in the "top 20."

The newly wealthy Asians like to be on a list, preferably as "Number 1." And there are lists. The *Forbes* 2014 Billionaires list (a total of 444 names) lists the "top three" Asians (all from Hong Kong): Li Ka-shing (#20), Lui Che Woo (#28) and Lee Shau Kee (#35).

People on the *Forbes* list are not only wealthy, the wealth makes them very important: "[T]his year's Asian list [is] worth a careful look for readers interested in what's ahead in global business, where to invest and where to sell goods and services."

Latin

Continuing our focus on Latin families from countries with widespread kidnapping, being on a "top" list is clearly dangerous.

Even the media does not report a "bragging" list. Instead the headline of the 2014 Oxfam report on rich Latin Americans has an accusing tone: "Annual income of the 113 richest people in Latin America could lift 25 million out of poverty." The number of billionaires by country: "(65 Brazilians, 16 Mexicans, 12 Chileans, 8 Peruvians, 5 Argentineans, 4 Colombians and 3 Venezuelans)."

When these families move themselves or their assets into a place like the United States they are likely to pick up the local customs that will include a justified and relaxed pride and enjoyment of their wealth.

Gulf

Within the Gulf region there are annual rankings by country. The *Forbes* 2014 "richest countries" list ranks Qatar as #1 and the UAE as #6. The

"London Rich List" includes from the Gulf only King Abdullah and Prince Al-Waleed (who actually sued *Forbes* in 2013 for understating his wealth). The *Forbes* list does not include King Abdullah. It has a policy of not including rulers. It also cannot give very accurate rankings in the Gulf as so much wealth is "in a family" and Forbes will only count individuals.

Among individuals in the Gulf, we have not heard comments of either "bragging" or of "envy." In fact, most families seem to have only a vague idea of their net worth. (One exception was a staff man for a Saudi Prince—he wanted to brag about how large the home was [50,000 square feet]—we doubt the Prince would have liked that.)

CHAPTER SIX

"Sally says she'll get a new charm bracelet if she gets an A in math. What will you give me?"

We might be in the minority, but to us this approach with children is a guaranteed "lose-lose." Why?

Goals are good for us all.

Rewards? Bribes? It's a tough question for all parents. But when money gets involved it adds to the confusion.

Going back to basics, what behavior is being encouraged? Is it consistent with the child's talents? The next question is how to encourage that behavior.

Either the child is able to get the "A" or she is not. Let's look at what the promise of a reward, of a bracelet or of money, adds to the equation. What does a child learn from this use of money?

The young children see their older brothers and sisters being promised cars, jewelry and vacations, on conditions of performance. "If you get above "X" on your SAT scores, we will give you a car." "If your grades are good, we will give you a ski vacation." "If you get into Harvard or Yale, we will donate a wing to the school."

A true benefit of wealth may be the luxury to do whatever you really want. How extra fortunate if you have been raised to look for and be proud of your own special talents, whatever they may be.

Does this child like math? Could she use some help? Is her friend having a hard time in math?

Look for, and support all of the natural abilities of your child—help your child learn to shine, and to take great enjoyment from the use of her or his talents.

Of course children always seem to "want" something and parents love to make children happy. The money issue of this chapter is the difficulty of using money as a reward in itself.

On the other hand, another luxury of wealth is to be able to give special treats to children just because you want them to enjoy it. The charm bracelet admired because it jangles in a pretty way can be a lovely gift-just-because-you're-you.

So, back to her question: "What will you give me?"

LESSON

How about one of these:

- "I don't need to give you anything. You will feel so good about yourself—that will be your best reward!"

- "We will all be so proud of how hard you worked!"

- "You can choose a special gift for "Toys for Tots" or the pet shelter, etc."

Age 12:

Even at age 12, the child can tell that this chapter is really about rewards and bribes! It also introduces the idea of having money (or rewards) withheld if the behavior does not meet the required standard.

We are convinced, from our work with families, that to connect the use of money to a child's behavior sets the stage for a life-long confusion of money with personal worth. One 70-year-old still remembers being

told at age 12 by his father that he was a negative financial drain on the family and should keep track of his meals and costs in order to pay it all back someday.

On the other hand, some children do like the idea of having "something" to look forward to, and it doesn't need to be money or expensive bracelets—it could be going out for ice cream, or having friends for a sleep over.

Children want to flourish and to learn to use their talents well; parents can encourage them without resorting to financial bribes or rewards. The pride in achievement speaks for itself in a supportive family.

Age 20:

At this age the bribes and rewards often become more complicated. At the simple end is the promise of a new car upon graduation—if the grades are good.

More complicated are the strings attached to family trust provisions—the most extreme example being the use of an "incentive" trust. Under these trusts the distribution of money is directly tied to satisfactory performance of the behaviors (grades, jobs, clean drug tests, etc.) written into the trust document. This is not a way to learn, share and explain family values.

The ultimate threat (in those countries where it is possible to do so, which includes the United States) is to disinherit a child. One long-term married couple will never forget the groom's father threatening to cut his son out of his will if he proceeded to get married at a stage in his career that his father felt was not suitable.

Parents could also keep in mind that controlling the child's behavior might not give the child the freedom to make mistakes and to learn from their failures. To recover from failures builds stronger, more resilient young adults.

GLOBAL NUANCES

Asian

In many Asian families the pressure that parents put on their children to succeed at all costs gets enforced by adding on rewards (bribes) and threats. These apply to grades especially. In some cases Japanese parents, for example, have sent their children to Australia for school, just to escape the peer pressure about grades.

Latin

The close family ties in most Latin societies have led more to an attitude of encouraging children to do well as part of the values of the families, not to be collecting rewards.

As the families expand and members have different roles, there will be a mixture of successes and failures. The level of communication needs to increase. Each different path and venture needs to be respected—they are all part of the growth of the extended family.

Gulf

A number of Gulf families do give "rewards" for school performance, but not in order to "bribe" them. Bribing has the flavor of forcing a child to do something he or she would not really want to do. The Gulf rewards are more in the nature of celebrations, with the extended family. Those celebrations can apply to any sort of goal achieved, including those set by the child.

CHAPTER SEVEN

"But I want it!" and "But I want to!"

From ages 2 to 20 (or 30, or 40?) children are full of demands.

- "But Daddy, everyone else has one."
- "You have enough money to buy it for me."
- " I just need some extra money for a while, please."

Some parents have been rueful about the breadth of choices that money does offer. One father said, "I wish we could say no for a simple reason, like other people can, like "Sorry, it costs too much" or "We just can't afford it." But his son knows that he can afford it, so he has to work harder for a reason.

Working harder for reasons can be a great opportunity to talk through family values. We'll talk more in another chapter about ways that families give to communities, but one example fits well here.

"Our daughter saw the gift we were giving to her elementary school, so we had an opportunity to talk about that gift, which everyone would know about, and also tell her that we make many gifts that are "anonymous" because that is a value that Grandpa and Grandma started. That is something that is important in our family."

Many families have "dodged" this difficult parental role of talking about values that lead to decisions by falling back on the institution of a trust.

Compare how this answer sounds to a child:

"We would have to ask the Trustee about that, and it may
not be appropriate under the terms of the trust agreement."

We know that young children do not understand this one at all, just that their own mother or father says someone else makes those decisions.

If a bank is a Trustee, the buffer is often a strong one. In one case, the bank trust officer called one of us (paying for legal fees, from the trust funds) to ask whether it would be appropriate to comply with a 60 year-old primary beneficiary's request for money for a fur coat for herself! Banks need their own internal "committee approval" for any significant trust distribution.

As one mother who married a man who had grown up with trusts commented:

"We have been kept prisoner by my husband's trusts.
I could never put my children through that."

Forcing someone else's judgment on children can become a life-long habit, as the woman in the above quote knew all too well. This really can last a long time.

One client came in saying:

"My father set this trust up for me, but now I'm already 70 years old. I am old enough to handle my own money. Can you help me?"

As children get older, premarital agreements can also be used (but certainly do not have to be) to impose someone else's judgment. If the message is:"We don't trust your judgment in having chosen this future spouse, so we will "take care of you," then the "child" is not able to feel like a mature, respected individual.

Instead if the child has developed a good sense of family values, the premarital agreement could be used in a positive way to ensure protection of family assets.

Teaching children early about patience, delay and priorities are extremely valuable lessons. Teaching children about family values is a wonderful way to shape their own character, as they grow up and as they have their own children. These are lessons they will remember!

- "I knew that my allowance would be used one-third for myself, one-third for savings, and one-third to give to those who needed it more."

- "My grandmother taught me that a few well-chosen clothes could be worn for many, many years."

- "We all spend our vacation time at the old family cabins up at the lake. It's quiet and primitive, but we love it."

LESSON

Try answering those "I want it" and "I want to" questions as follows:

- "Do you want to use some of the money you saved to pay for half of it?"

- "Do you want to add that to the list of what you want, and we can look at the whole list on Saturday and choose one or two?"

- "Is there anything else that you would be happy doing instead?"

Age 12

All 12-year-olds understand "Immediate gratification." This is an age of seemingly constant demands relating to spending money. This also means it is a prime age for discussing and sharing very important family values. It is also a time for some emotional reactions to being denied whatever the child wants "now."

The opportunities to discuss the use of money are rich at this age, especially because the parent does control access to funds.

Unhelpful replies to "I want it now" include "No, you can't have it. Why? Because I said so." and "We can't afford it" or "It costs too much." The first approach ("because I said so") leaves the child shut down in terms of any learning about values. The second approach ("it costs too much") is not believable in a wealthy family.

The more helpful approach is to say that "I do not think it has enough value right now because....." and to start a dialogue. One mother in a wealthy family said that being wealthy made it so difficult to say "no" to a child's purchase demands because they all knew that the reason "we can't afford it" simply was not true.

One woman worked hard to teach her 12-year-old granddaughter the value of being patient when they were out shopping. The girl had been promised a dress, and they couldn't find one they both liked. The girl hurried at the end and said she'd take an orange "cheaply made" one, to have it "now." Facing an all-out tantrum the grandmother insisted that the girl would have to wait until the next day and they would try again. They did find a perfect (and well-made) dress. Even better is the lesson in values—the granddaughter has since been reminded "remember that time you waited for a better dress?"

Age 20

By the time a child reaches age 20 we hope the parents realize that the critical values relating to money have already been established. Assuming there are no restrictive trusts controlling the access to money, it is quite likely that at this age they do have independent access to funds.

One 20-year-old announced to her parents during a college break that she and a girlfriend planned to spend a summer traveling around Europe. The parents were very opposed, worried about the safety of the two girls, and explained that they would not give their permission. "Too bad," said the girl, "I have my own money, we're going, and I'll send you postcards."

Another 20-something who joined the family business in a senior management position, insisted that he have a much larger office. His father had meant to save that for a few years. But when he listened to his son, he understood that the larger office would help at work to illustrate his position and reinforce to other employees that they should be reporting to him, not to his father.

As with so many other questions, this is a great opportunity to teach family values. Instead of closing the door with a "no" the parent can ask "Why do you want it" and then listen and learn.

GLOBAL NUANCES

Asian

As a culture many Asians are accustomed to waiting and to having patience. Recently the children of the newly wealthy are less adapted to the concept of waiting, and are more in the mode of wanting it "now."

Latin

In the context of a large extended family, the individual child has a sense of community, with the reassurance that brings. We think that reassurance also promotes a patience—that part of the lesson in the family environment is that important stages will happen, all in due course.

We also see that reassurance supporting an attitude toward risks that is another key lesson in patience. The goal may not have been reached today, but there is always tomorrow.

As the families become more globalized, they need to learn how to navigate among different cultures. This skill can take years to learn—so learning patience early will be very valuable later.

Gulf

Gulf families who have "unlimited" family wealth do not see a moral issue about going ahead and having what they want now. At the same time this comes more from a nature of generosity than from a selfishness. For example, visitors to the Gulf learn early that the risk of admiring a book or a painting is that it will be handed over to the visitor to keep.

CHAPTER EIGHT

"I might be rich when I grow up... how much money does a ballerina get?"

We asked our informal volunteers to answer a question about their future: "Will you have a lot of money when you grow up?"

- Yes...

- Maybe...

- And one ballerina

Let's think about the little ballerina. One of the benefits of wealth is having choices and freedom. Many comment that that is also one of the disadvantages.

One man wanted to explain, thinking of many friends he had seen, that:

"When you don't have to do anything...you might not."

He said that in those circumstances:

"It takes a tremendous inner discipline to work to achieve goals, and even to set those goals."

Passive wealth is looked down upon by most Americans, as mentioned in the early part of this book. The recipients did nothing to "earn" it. Parents worry that their own children will not be seen as a success in light of those values. Children figure that out, of course, and feel a lack of their own self-worth.

Today there is a popular rallying cry by the new self-made financial-successes, they do not want to give "too much" to their children. So the question for them becomes, "How much is too much?"

Warren Buffett is often quoted by other financially successful people who love his line:

"I want to give my children enough, so they can do anything, but not so much that they can do nothing."

A tax lawyer agrees and urges clients to give more to charity and less to children:

"Do not deprive your children of the opportunity to learn how to work hard and make their own money."

This only makes sense if everyone agrees that:

- Money is the important "scorecard"

- Traditional work-for-money is the only recognized path to valued success

- Earning money is the right way to use our talents

Back to the ballerina....This young girl feels just great thinking of herself as an artist. Money is an add-on. She knows she will be a ballerina. She answers our question in those terms: yes, she might have a lot of money, it depends on how much ballerinas make. Or not.

But it won't be the money that will change her decision to be a ballerina.
She is fortunate to be growing up in a family that has enough financial

resources so that she can be anything that she chooses to be. Her parents are thrilled.

We usually answer the chapter heading question at this point, and she did ask a question (How much money do ballerinas make?), but we don't think she cared about getting any answers to that question. Do you?

Look at how people have written about dance!

"To dance is to be out of yourself, larger, more powerful, more beautiful. This is power, it is glory on earth and it is yours for the taking."
—AGNES DE MILLE

"We ought to dance with rapture that we might be alive...and part of the living, incarnate cosmos."
—D. H. LAWRENCE

and

"We should consider every day lost on which we have not danced at least once."
—FRIEDRICH WILHELM NIETZSCHE

Age 12

A clever 12-year-old might answer this question with a question: "why are you asking me that, what does being rich have to do with doing what I want to do?"

It is more likely though that the child will by now have adopted the value that "to be rich" is a good goal to have. Parents can help by stepping in with comments many adults remember as being their best motivator in life: "My parents always said I could be anything I wanted to be." When this message is given to a child with love and encouragement, it inspires the child to evaluate all of the possibilities and choose his or her own.

One father stressed to his 12-year-old son that he should never sign anything that he did not understand. As a lesson the father prepared a "Consent" for all the children to sign, that included their agreement to discontinue allowances. The 12-year-old was the only one who didn't sign.

One family office in the United States is concentrating on the 4th generation and providing training and educational counselors on many topics, all with the goal of making them able to live "independent of the family money."

In terms of being rich, one girl warns "You shouldn't spend too much money or you won't be rich anymore."

Age 20

This is an age to reinforce the family values that have gone into the young adult's character development. It is a great age for extended conversations.

One cynical 20-year-old told her father there was no reason to hang out the American flag: "It's a country that had slavery, Japanese camps and still discriminates." Instead of scolding her, the father told her that in the history of their family, who had escaped from Europe, it was a place of hope and freedom. He took away the comforting thought that he had at least made a gift to her of "a different perspective." This was a gift that serves her well today.

The gift of having family wealth allows a young adult to "follow your dream" and not be restricted to vocations that earn well. As John Adams, a founding Father of the United States explained:

> "I must study politics and war, that our sons may have liberty to study mathematics and philosophy. Our sons ought to study mathematics and philosophy, geography, natural history and naval architecture, navigation, commerce and agriculture in order to give their children a right to study painting, poetry, music, architecture, statuary, tapestry and porcelain."

To be able to use one's special talents, whatever they are, to work to improve and to enjoy the process, this is what a leading academic found to be "the good life." (Professor Mihaly Csikszentmihalyi, author of the book *Flow*, about the meaning of a good life).

GLOBAL NUANCES

Asian

As a new generation becomes successful, and has been pressured to attain that success, at some point they will pause and ask "is this all?" and "is this the purpose of life?" They may tap into the wisdom of Confucius and seek to deepen their personal peace and family peace. One advisor to Asian families encourages them to re-emphasize the wisdom that can come from the elders in the family.

Latin

For the families that have relocated away from their home country, much of their effort must go into managing this enormous change. To succeed will become a priority. Satisfaction comes from managing the talents of the entire family. To be able to preserve some (but usually not all) of the original family wealth will count as success. So will being able to work together.

As family members relocate, the nuclear family unit may become more focused on the wealth that will be needed by the nuclear family, not by the extended family back home. The new environment might cause some new hesitancy, with a new need to ask themselves about the effect on their lifestyle.

Gulf

The sense of happiness in a Gulf family seems to revolve around the family. Many of the families are quite large, giving increased numbers of people to watch over and care about. An individual is probably as happy as the entire family is happy (or not). With a religious acceptance ("Allah will provide") and a reminder of the intrinsic dangers in life, by the constant use, when making plans, of the word "enshallah" (Allah so providing), the family appreciates the good times.

CHAPTER NINE

"If Daddy divorces us, can I still go to camp this summer?"

For all of us money has some connection with security. Even the gov-
ernment "minimum" benefits are
called social "security," when you
think about it.

What are the security issues that
concern a young child? How does
money tie in? For a child in a house-
hold without much wealth, money is
a basic need. As one child said:

"Yes, money is good. It's your life. You can buy food."

Back in the communities our other quotes are from, "necessities" can
take on a very different meaning.

"Yes, money is good because it helps you pay for parking."

The insecurity about money, and its possible loss, is something that
often occurs in adults as well. One woman who had not worked during
her marriage to a very wealthy man became petrified after her separation.
During the several years of divorce negotiations she felt completely at risk.

"I can't afford to start a relationship with someone who does not have a lot of resources. I need to travel and to live a certain way."

Isn't this a later version of not being able to "go to camp"?

Children easily sense a parent's insecurities, of all kinds. If a parent who is insecure keeps giving a child a message, even unconsciously, that they need to worry about money, that it may run out, that they may not get more, or even that they are "poor"—the child will believe the parent. That's what children do.

One man mentioned that he was unaware of his daughter's conviction that she was "poor" until he overheard her explain to a friend of hers that she was "poor" when she was 15 years old! This child lived in a "gated community," replete with house and cars, and did volunteer work in an inner city. In other words, she had all the external information available to her about the economic spectrum for families. Hers was clearly near the top end, yet she believed what she had incorporated from her mother over the years. Of course, the mother was insecure, for whatever reason. It was passed on to her daughter.

It is fascinating, but true that someone can become so used to feeling financially insecure that the reasons that lead to that feeling are long forgotten. Many widows have been unconvinced by accountants' proofs that they could never spend their accumulated resources.

One retired wealthy man, without any special heirs for whom the wealth is being saved, is afraid to spend, or share, any of his money, needing to feel reassured that he will have a surplus at his death.

What is the child really worried about?

- Is it one more summer of camp?

- Are there special friends at camp?

- Or is it the disruption of life as she has known it?

Once you have thought about, and we hope talked about, what is really worrying them, maybe you can talk about those issues—which may have nothing at all to do with camp.

LESSON

Try one of the following.

- "You sound worried. What is it?"

- "Daddy and I love you very much. That will never change."

- "Would you like to invite one of your camp friends to come and visit for a while?"

Age 12

This chapter is about insecurity. When there is a drastic change in the family, or even when there is simply fear that such a change will happen, a 12-year-old is especially vulnerable. This is a time for solid reassurance.

Some changes are harder than others, and some can be controlled but others "just happen." Whether it is death, divorce, illness or moving, the child is likely to feel his or her world has lost its reliability and its predictability. The comfort of a familiar world is taken away.

One 12-year-old was shaken by a family relocation: what would happen if his school was taken away, and he had to go to a new one?

What children need throughout this is strong support and honest discussions. They can learn that yes, this is hard (or unfortunate or "not fair") but that the family can cope. To be encouraged to be resilient is to be given an important gift.

Age 20

At age 20 the child is ready to think about leaving home, which is change that could be negative or positive. Another big change at that age is thinking about living with someone else, as spouses or partners, with all the adjustments and surprises that come with that change.

Parents worry about their young adult children. This worry in a wealthy family is exaggerated by the fear that they will be taken advantage of, and perhaps even loved more for their money than for themselves (a fear often shared by the young adult). One solution is to create trusts for the child, to protect the wealth from "creditors and predators." Unless this is discussed with the child, the result is often a conviction by the child that they are simply "not trusted."

In some cases this is also an age where the adult child begins to worry about the parents or grandparents. Will there be medical conditions that will change their lives? Will their lifestyles be supportable indefinitely?

GLOBAL NUANCES

Asian

Looking still at the ethnic Chinese, those who have survived hard times on the mainland may keep the fear that all could change again. They wonder if they should obtain an additional passport (such as a Canadian one) or should they be sure to keep their wealth in a safe location. The luxury of owning private property is a new enough fact to bring with it some insecurity, rational or not.

Latin

When family members spend a lot of individual time in different countries, there is a confusion of values for the children. The father may be in a Latin country most of the time, with his business, while the mother is caring for the children in a new country. The unity of the family becomes diluted and disjointed. These changes are hard on their own, when mixed from several global sources they are even more challenging. Families need to work harder to keep the unity.

Gulf

Some families across the Gulf Region, especially after the Arab Spring and the ISIS movement, are concerned about long-term stability in the region. Families also remember nationalizations (and the partition in India) and often like to keep some offshore accounts, just in case. Some are even creating trusts to be based offshore, as a safety net for their future generations.

CHAPTER TEN

"Can we bring Annie
with us on our vacation?"

What if the vacation is quite expensive and Annie's parents would not be able to pay for her share?

When and how does a child learn to share?

Will that child grow up wanting to share in a number of ways—with family, friends and the rest of the world?

One of the most touching stories we heard was from a woman who began with a small simple "Baby Hannukah" party for her own very young grandchildren. The party was in her home and her children invited some of their own friends and their little children.

- Everyone had lots of fun and the next year the party group had outgrown the home and had its celebration in the nearby Lutheran Church.

- Each little child was asked to bring a gift for an "underprivileged" child in the area—at the Catholic-sponsored Children's Foundling Home.

- She still is amazed when she describes how much children as young as 3 had understood "sharing" and how much they looked forward to it.

We get very excited about the uses of philanthropy to involve children and to teach and pass on family values.

Another lovely approach to teaching children about "sharing" is to work with a family foundation.

All around the country families are becoming much more active in the operations of their family foundations.

In the old days, family foundation operations were a pretty simple, and passive process. Charities sent solicitation requests all during the year. They were neatly placed in a stack. Near the end of the year, the patriarch (or matriarch) would go through the pile and choose the ones to whom checks would be sent that year. Not much else was involved.

Today, we find families very involved, with the entire family included, in discussions about:

- the foundation's mission statement,

- the specific areas of focus for the family's giving,

- the formation of specialized committees,

- financial projections and investment strategies,

- preparation of RFPs (requests for proposals),

- board membership, and

- succession governance plans.

For many young adults the family foundation can give them their first meaningful, respected role in the family group. This can do wonders for self-esteem and skill building.

Note: For a searchable internet listing of all foundations, you might enjoy browsing through the <www.guidestar.org> site. You will find several family foundations that have created their own web sites. Our favorites are the ones that include some of the family history, with photos too.

So very positive lessons can come from how a family uses some of its wealth in giving to the rest of the world.

One caution though: many who are newly wealthy are convinced (see our history chapter) that too much money will automatically ruin their children (e.g. they won't work for a living) and for that reason alone have decided that a major portion of their wealth will go to charity.

Children who get the message they can't be trusted will never feel the same. Why not consider the values the children do have? If the children have been raised to live wisely with wealth: to earn and save and give, why not trust them to continue those family values and to create their own satisfactions from giving, which they will pass on to their children and to their children's children...?

If it does make sense to give a major portion to charity, why not explain the reasons for that decision with the children in the family?

If the messages are positive, and communicated, the negative effects we have seen should never occur in the first place.

In fact, we know a few special families where the decision to focus predominately on giving to others, often for a special cause, was discussed and agreed upon by the entire family—including all the children. Foundations that are used in all these ways can bring a family together—across the generations—and can keep a family together for future generations.

Today, those children who grew up with an involvement in their family foundation, and who are now adults, have felt a lasting enjoyment from their special family legacy.

Whatever the family tradition is, teaching young children—very young children—to "share" is a gift to them of a life-long rewarding value.

LESSON

Back to Annie and the vacation...How about answering the question with one of these?

- "Would you like to share some of your allowance for Annie to come?"
- "We would be glad to share our time with Annie and you."

- "We will talk to her parents about how we can share the vacation." [Note: They might want to share some part of the costs, too]

This chapter is about sharing, but with the complexities that come with unequal wealth.

Age 12

The questions range from sharing sports equipment to exchanging dresses, or even just shopping together.

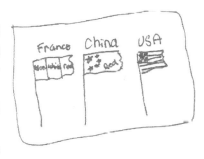

One child may be able to spend easily, and have "the best" of every thing. The friend may have much less. When there is a natural urge to share, at what point does it become embarrassing to—or resented by— the friend who has much less?

In terms of sharing vacations, one girl explained that she really wanted her Dad to include her best friend on a trip to Italy because "she's never been outside the United States." The reply was a "maybe" (the girl thinks that means it won't happen). Her next argument will be that she can share her hotel room, so they won't have to pay for another one.

We can imagine that not all friends' parent will feel secure about a child being "treated" to such a generous vacation.

Sometimes generosity is not welcomed.

Age 20

The major issue about sharing financial wealth comes at the time of marriage. Will it be "share and share alike?" Or will it be "my accounts" and "your accounts?" As mentioned before the fact of signing a prenuptial is to legalize the limits of sharing.

Related issues are less serious but have the common theme of encouraging the child not to share, just in case the friendship (or love) is in part caused by an attraction to the wealth that would be shared. Parents often try to protect their adult children from others who are eager to share in the wealth.

One man in his 60s looks back and realizes: "The worst value that was passed on to me was to not trust anyone."

He would gladly have preferred to be tricked by someone he should not have trusted—than to spend his life avoiding sharing whenever possible.

GLOBAL NUANCES

On this topic we were stumped. Every time we thought of one possible generalization we thought of exceptions. In the end, we decided that how and what families share with others is very family-specific. Some easily share everything with everyone; others distrust all outsiders and would not consider sharing anything with anyone.

CHAPTER ELEVEN

"If you won't let me have it, I'll call Grandma."

We sing to little babies the old lullaby:

"Hush, little baby, don't say a word.
Papa's gonna buy you a mockingbird

And if that mockingbird won't sing,
Papa's gonna buy you a diamond ring

And if that diamond ring turns brass,
Papa's gonna buy you a looking glass

And if that looking glass gets broke,
Papa's gonna buy you a billy goat

And if that billy goat won't pull,
Papa's gonna buy you a cart and bull

And if that cart and bull fall down,
You'll still be the sweetest little baby in town."

Notice that the love is expressed in what would be bought. Children quickly catch on to this characteristic of money.

- Money can't buy you love, or can it?

- Can taking it away, take away love?

- Does it matter who the recipient would be?

- Does the motive matter?

All the parents who work diligently so "my kids will not have to struggle the way I did" are expressing a deep human desire—to leave a legacy for the good of their children. With trust funds and other investments those same motives apply.

What can be different is when the freely given nature is changed to using money as a tool of manipulation. As one recipient adult remarked: "If I had known that gift had a price attached I might not have wanted it in the first place."

That equation leads to "He who has the gold makes the rule." It's another form of the little boy who takes a bag of candy to the school playground, to get friends.

"There are three great friends: an old wife,
an old dog, and ready money."

—BENJAMIN FRANKLIN

Many do develop a habit of giving money to "buy" love and taking it away to "punish." Those children become used to that and often continue those same habits when they are adults.

At the time of writing down what will be left to children at the end of one's life, many clients have tried to make a rational allocation based on need. One child may have become quite successful but the other two would still appreciate the extra resources, thinks the parent.

No matter how thoughtful and conscientious the parent was in that decision, the child who hears in a Will that he has been disinherited will often hear the following language:

"To my son John I leave nothing, not because of any lack of affection, but because he has sufficient resources..."

> *No matter how many resources John has, he will be deeply hurt. It will feel like a lack of affection, the worst kind of all because it can never been undone.*

One man was hurt, not for himself but for his own children. Their grandfather had died and had left nothing to them (not even a token tied to affection). He was aggrieved enough to challenge the Will.

> *"My father didn't mention my children in his Will, and they loved going fishing with him. They thought he loved them."*

To that man, his father should have left something or else the grandchildren would believe that he had never loved them.

> *Those children didn't understand that spending his time with them was a way that their grandfather was showing them his love for them.*

Although this is a sad example of an ingrained belief that love is shown by money, it also would have been a simple one to accommodate. Those grandchildren would probably have cherished a collection of favorite fishing rods.

Mixing money with love leads to the spending on toys, tennis lessons and later cars. One teenager had the pleasure of being given an $80,000 car, but he usually ate dinner all alone. His parents were too busy to spend time with him.

———

One mother said she was so pleased:

"Our son is having his 24th birthday and we'll be able to spend it with him. We've always had a gala or something to go to before. This will be the first time we can spend his birthday with him."

We all know men who never had time to spend with their children, but now they have a new, second family and they make the time. More than one CEO has cut his business trip short hoping to get back in time to watch his 10 year-old's soccer game.

One grown daughter is still hurt:

"I was a violinist in our school orchestra and my father never came to see me play—not once. He said he was too busy making money for us."

Back to the Grandma who is the child's back up plan. One caution is to keep the parental role clear and active. Children can learn quite young, how to encourage the grandparents to "take their side" when the parents say "no." The "end run" around the parents teaches the child that a certain lack of respect for the parents is approved, and even fruitful. We find many parents who would like to be more involved in discussing the grandparents' plans for the young children. If the parents have been working on values, and patience and priorities, they do not want to have that all undone by a generous trust.

The grandparents, on the other hand, are not responsible for the teaching lessons that are part of raising the child. They are at a stage when they just love giving.

One young father discussed this with the grandparents and together they arrived at a trust provision that said:

"Distributions to the children while they are under age 21 need to be discussed by the Trustees with the child's parents prior to making any such distribution."

This was a way of letting the Trustees know that the grandparents'
wishes were to include and respect the values and opinions of the parents.
One dear little girl knew all about grandparents:

"When you get old you get money, and
little spots on your arms."

LESSON

- The grandparents who "side with" young children, using money as a tool, and let them go around the parents' expressed wishes are teaching the children that they do not have to listen to, or respect, their parents.

- There are special bonds between grandparents and grandchildren—and this can be wonderful for everyone.

- If the grandparents and parents can enjoy their separate roles ("At Grandma's you can eat peanut butter for breakfast, but not here. Yes, Grandpa lets you bang on the piano, but not here." And so on.) in "harmony" with each other, everyone can enjoy the role they have in the child's life. Even money can be given!

Age 12:

By that age a child has already figured out that the Grandparent pitch is not a sure thing. One child explained very seriously "Since my grandmother manages money I think she'd say no." She has also become wiser about understanding her "wants." "Its probably something that is so-so anyway, that I don't really want. So I should just move on, and wait until there's something I really want." Also, she adds (having learned the patience lesson) "maybe later I could get it."

Age 20:

By this age the young adult often has enough confidence to have thought through his or her needs and desires. There can be a genuine difference of views between them and their parents. In some cases the child might think it is fair to go to the grandparents and ask their opinions. This is also an age when they are likely to be receiving annual gifts from grandparents—as part of estate planning. Grandparents everywhere like to be thanked! This could also open a discussion about estate planning.

GLOBAL NUANCES

Asian

In Asian families age brings respect. Children learn to be careful and polite before making any requests to their elders. The opinion of the elders also matters a great deal: the child would not want to appear selfish or petty or nagging.

Any advice offered by a grandparent would command acceptance. This gives a grandparent a great opportunity to reinforce family values.

Latin

As with the Asian families, the position of the elders in the family carries with it great respect. This means that advice (and wisdom) offered by a grandparent would be considered very seriously, and would have a great impact. That bond is a great way to keep passing on family values.

Gulf

In the extended family the pressure to be agreeable is a strong one. Dissenters need to consider their opinions carefully before raising disagreements. As with Asian families the opinion of the elders will carry very strong weight. In some cases that weight is tied to the control of the family wealth.

CHAPTER TWELVE

"So Mommy, are we rich?"

Now that we've been through all those other questions...what have we learned?

- We know that children have different reasons for asking questions...and it helps to know their reasons.

- We know that children have different kinds of questions at different ages....and need different kinds of answers for each age.

- We know that children are growing up in families that have their own special values about money...and the children want to learn those and be part of them.

How about these closing thoughts:

- Money is. . .Just Money.

Not an end in itself, not a value in itself, not the one scorecard in life, and not any of the other assumptions. It is simply a neutral medium of exchange.

Money is what you and your family make of it!

And, last but most important, children want to understand money, just as they want to understand everything else!

Closing Thoughts

We noticed how often we mentioned that a topic presented a "great opportunity to have a discussion." That seems to be our overall theme.

Our general advice is to keep communicating with your children on these issues. We know that the family wealth issues are hard ones for many parents. One thoughtful father has explained that the difficulties really stem from the parent's own conflicting views about family wealth. He advises trying to sort out the adult views better, to raise children with healthier views on family wealth. One way to clarify an adult's views on family wealth is actually to try answering the questions asked by children, like the questions in this book.

We think the best way to do this is to keep talking with your children (of all ages), in a very honest way, sharing whatever your actual views are about family wealth. Sharing these views, in a way that welcomes dialogues, will also strengthen the bonds and trust and understanding between parents and their children.

We wish you the very best!

About the Authors

Barbara Hauser is an internationally recognized advisor to global families. She is invited to speak at leading family wealth events around the world, and enjoys working with complex families on family governance, family offices, family business continuity, offshore trusts and the coordination of generational transitions.

Publications include:"Creating Family Governance Systems in Different Cultures," "Successful Family Business (and Wealth) Transitions: Next Generation Involvement Improves the Odds," "The Four Seasons of Sustainable Wealth," "Family Office Trends: Lessons from Dubai?," "Family Governance: Who, What and How," "Appreciating Beneficiaries," "How to Interview a Corporate Trustee" and "The Next Generation and the Pursuit of Happiness." Books include *Mommy, are we rich?: Talking to Children about Family Money, International Estate Planning: A Reference Guide, You Have to Change at Poggibonsi,* and *International Family Governance.*

After Wellesley College, and the University of Pennsylvania Law School, Barbara had the high honor of clerking at the U.S. Supreme Court, and then was a partner in law firms, a law school professor, and an executive with global investment firms. She is now an independent family advisor, with clients in Europe, Saudi Arabia and Asia.

www.brhauser.com

Suzy Peterfriend Ross, founder and president of Family Legacy, Inc. is based in South Florida.

Suzy draws upon her extensive background as an advisor and consultant, in addition to her experience in her own family's business. She helps stateside families with international business interests develop governance and strategies for intergenerational wealth transfers.

Suzy is the co-founder (with Barbara Hauser) of the Family Advisory Council, formed in 1996 to give both family members and their advisors a way to have confidential discussions in a private and secure setting. The Council was nominated in 2005 for "Family Group of the Year," by the High Net Worth Industry Awards Program and continues to meet in New York. In 2007 Suzy extended the concept and formed an international group in Miami for Latin American families.

Currently she works with a number of families from the Americas who are in transition to live as residents stateside.

She is the author of "Life Is Short Art Is Long: Maximizing Estate Planning Strategies for Collectors of Art, Antiques, and Collectibles" (Wealth Management Press, 2007) and writes innovative articles on issues surrounding wealth transfers. She was a guest on Wealth and Wisdom at WXEL, South Florida's NPR affiliate. Hobbies include entering equestrian events with her granddaughter, one of the illustrators.